Desserts from Around the World

An Imprint of Pop!
popbooksonline.com

DEEP-FRIED DESSERTS
FROM AROUND THE WORLD

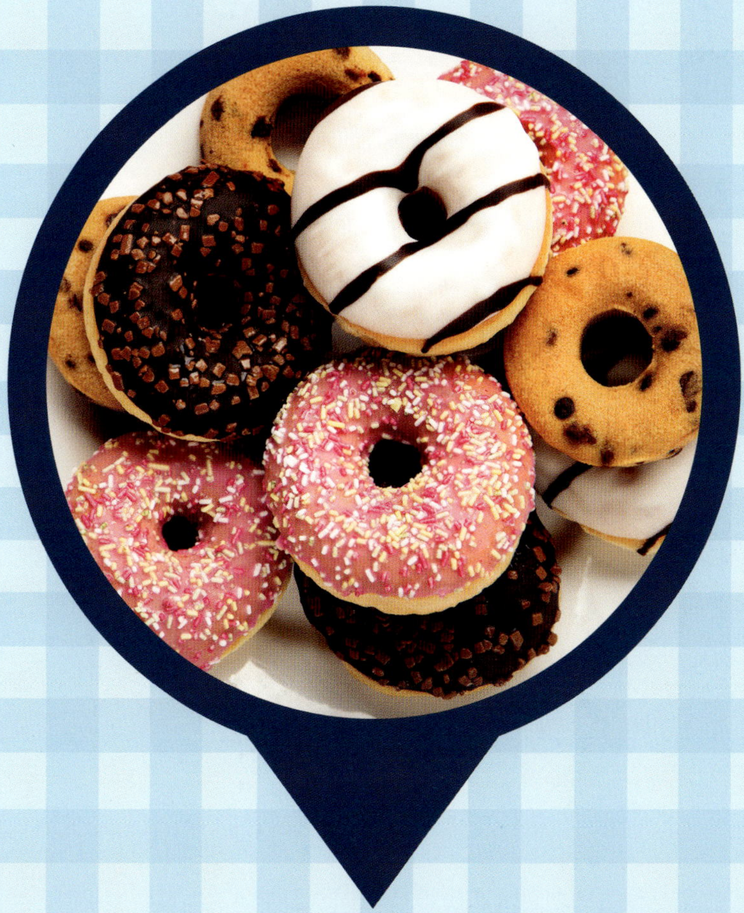

by Grace Hansen

WELCOME TO DiscoverRoo!

This book is filled with videos, puzzles, games, and more! Scan the QR codes* while you read, or visit the website below to make this book pop.

popbooksonline.com/deep-fried

abdobooks.com

Published by Pop!, a division of ABDO, PO Box 398166, Minneapolis, Minnesota 55439. Copyright © 2025 by Abdo Consulting Group, Inc. International copyrights reserved in all countries. No part of this book may be reproduced in any form without written permission from the publisher. DiscoverRoo™ is a trademark and logo of Pop!.

Printed in the United States of America, North Mankato, Minnesota.

102024
012025

THIS BOOK CONTAINS RECYCLED MATERIALS

Cover Photo: Getty Images
Interior Photos: Shutterstock Images, Getty Images
Editor: Elizabeth Andrews
Series Designer: Laura Graphenteen

Library of Congress Control Number: 2024938598

Publisher's Cataloging-in-Publication Data
Names: Hansen, Grace, author.
Title: Deep-fried desserts from around the world / by Grace Hansen
Description: Minneapolis, Minnesota : Pop!, 2025 | Series: Desserts from around the world | Includes online resources and index
Identifiers: ISBN 9781098247126 (lib. bdg.) | ISBN 9781098247683 (ebook)
Subjects: LCSH: Baking--Juvenile literature. | Desserts--Juvenile literature. | Baked products--Juvenile literature. | Deep frying--Juvenile literature. | Cooking (Canola oil)--Juvenile literature. | Cookery--Juvenile literature.
Classification: DDC 641.77--dc23

*Scanning QR codes requires a web-enabled smart device with a QR code reader app and a camera.

TABLE OF CONTENTS

CHAPTER 1
The History of Dessert............ 4

CHAPTER 2
Deep-Fried Desserts
from Europe..................... 10

CHAPTER 3
Deep-Fried Desserts
from the Americas................16

CHAPTER 4
Deep-Fried Desserts
from Asia and Africa............. 20

More Deep-Fried Desserts
from Around the World!.......... 28
Making Connections............. 30
Glossary 31
Index & Online Resources 32

CHAPTER 1

THE HISTORY OF DESSERT

Desserts can be traced back to ancient times. The Mesopotamians had a fruitcake-like recipe. The Ancient Egyptians sweetened round, flat breads with dates and honey and cooked them over hot stones.

WATCH A VIDEO HERE!

Much of what we know about the Ancient Egyptians comes from wall paintings in temples and tombs.

The shape celebrated the sun and moon.

The Ancient Romans enjoyed simple sweet treats such as fruits, honey cakes, and fruit tarts.

This English oil painting from 1867 shows a first birthday celebration with cake and a candle.

In the 7th century, Persia (now Iran) was one of the first to harvest sugar cane and make cake-like cookies. In the 1500s, sugar became more affordable and widely available. In 1596, a cookbook was published for the growing middle classes in England. In it was a recipe for Fine Cakes. Later, Europeans made it more common to serve dessert, especially cake, for special occasions such as weddings.

Between 800 and 900, the Persians brought sugar cane to Southern Europe.

To this day, desserts help people around the world start the day, complete a meal, and celebrate important **milestones** and holidays. Let's go around the world and learn about deep-fried desserts from different places and **cultures**!

Almond cake, such as the one in this Ancient Roman mosaic, would have required a great amount of effort to prepare.

Mochi has long been enjoyed in Japan to celebrate the New Year. It was said to harden the teeth and therefore extend life.

CHAPTER 2
DEEP-FRIED DESSERTS FROM EUROPE

A lot happened in France in the 17th century, including many **crises**. But this period in France is also referred to as the "Great Century." One great thing to come from this time was the warm, fluffy, deep-fried Beignet (pronounced ben-YAY).

LEARN MORE HERE!

Unlike most donuts, Beignets are often square shaped.

Beignets can be filled with fruit jam.

Beignets are traditionally served hot, covered in powdered sugar, and paired with coffee. In the 18th century, French settlers came to New Orleans, Louisiana. They brought with them traditional foods from home, including Beignets. Today, Beignets are especially popular in the oldest neighborhood in New Orleans, the French Quarter.

FAT TUESDAY

Mardi Gras, French for "Fat Tuesday," is a Christian celebration that takes place every year before the start of Lent. Lent is traditionally a time when Christians **fast** and avoid rich foods. During Mardi Gras, people eat all of their favorite things. New Orleans hosts an annual festival. People gather and enjoy treats such as Beignets and sweet rice **fritters** called Calas.

The exact origin of Churros is debated, but many give credit to **shepherds** in Spain. The animal caretakers fried long strips of dough and coated them in sugar. These tasty treats were easy to carry through the mountains. Today, Churros are enjoyed throughout the world, especially in Latin America. Many people eat Churros along with dipping sauces, including chocolate and dulce de leche.

Churros are delicious with or without dipping sauces.

Some people believe that Churros were inspired by a popular, similarly-shaped 12th century Chinese food called youtiao.

CHAPTER 3

DEEP-FRIED DESSERTS FROM THE AMERICAS

A fried pastry called Picaron is beloved by Peruvians. The recipe was created with cost in mind. Traditional ancient ingredients, including squash and sweet potato, were affordable and readily available. Today, the recipe is much the same. The dough is shaped into rings

EXPLORE LINKS HERE!

Picarones originated in Lima, Peru, in the 1800s.

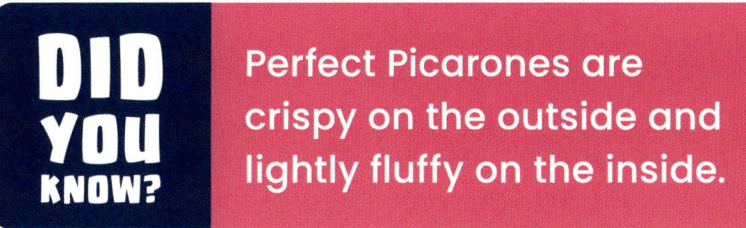

DID YOU KNOW? Perfect Picarones are crispy on the outside and lightly fluffy on the inside.

and fried in very hot oil. Picarones are then coated in a special syrup called *chancaca* and served hot.

The first BeaverTails location opened in 1980.

In 1978, Canadians Pam and Grant Hooker **debuted** their famous family recipe at a community fair in Killaloe, Ontario. It was a fried pastry the Hookers called "Beaver Tails." The couple would go on to open restaurants of the same name throughout Canada and other countries.

Beaver Tails are flat, oval-shaped donuts. The dough is **scored** in a square pattern to mimic the look of the animal's tail. Traditionally, the light, airy, and crispy donut is covered in cinnamon sugar. But there are plenty of other flavors to choose from!

Beaver Tail toppings can be sweet, salty, or savory.

CHAPTER 4

DEEP-FRIED DESSERTS FROM ASIA AND AFRICA

Kkwabaegi (pronounced kwa-be-gi), or Korean Twisted Donuts, can be traced back to a similar treat from ancient China called *mahua*. Kkwabaegi are spongy and slightly sweet. The dough is rolled into twisted ropes before deep frying. Once fried to perfection, the donuts are covered in sugar and cinnamon powder.

COMPLETE AN ACTIVITY HERE!

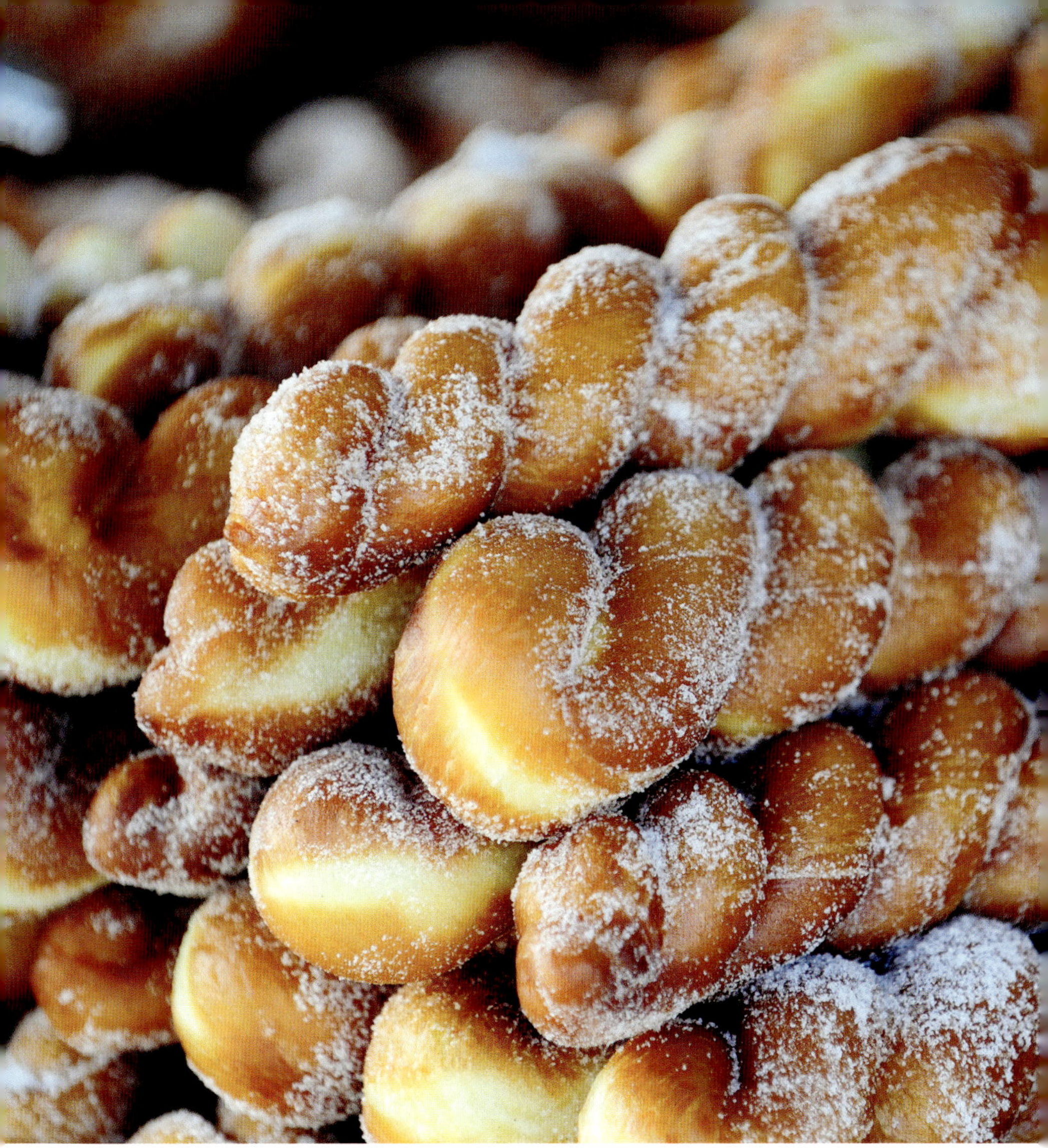

Kkwabaegi are best served hot and fresh!

DID YOU KNOW?

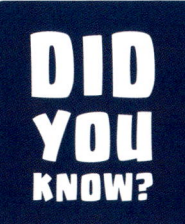

Kkwabaegi are a popular after-school snack in Korea.

(Top) *Bambalouni is very popular in the village of Sidi Bou Said;* (Bottom) *The donut is fried until golden brown.*

Tunisia is the northernmost country in Africa. It is famous for a sweet donut called Bambalouni. The donut is commonly served as street food or in shops, but it is also made at home. Bambalouni is finished with a sprinkle of sugar or a drizzle of honey. It can be enjoyed morning, noon, and night!

MOCHI DONUTS

Mochi Donuts are a type of dessert known as a fusion pastry. They are the combination of American-style donuts and Japanese Mochi. The pull-apart donut is formed using eight tiny balls made from a special batter. Mochi Donuts can be served plain, glazed, or rolled in brown sugar.

Puff Puff is a popular street food in Africa.

The Puff Puff is a popular and traditional treat served throughout West Africa. It is known by different names depending on the country. While it is made with basic ingredients, such as sugar, flour, and yeast, it is mouthwatering! The balls of dough are fried until they are golden-brown all over. To make Puff Puffs sweeter, they can be rolled in sugar or powdered sugar and served with jam.

Nigeria, Ghana, and Liberia are some countries where Puff Puff is often served.

Jalebi (juh-lay-be) is a popular treat in India and Pakistan. It is also eaten in other countries throughout Asia and Africa. The techniques to make it and its flavors differ from place to place. However, Jalebi is mainly made by deep

Jalebi dough must be thick enough to keep its shape, yet smooth enough to flow easily.

Jalebi is a celebration sweet in India. It is often made during Diwali, a Hindu holiday.

frying spiral-shaped dough and soaking it in sugar syrup. The treat is both crunchy and moist. Jalebi is served warm.

MORE DEEP-FRIED DESSERTS FROM AROUND THE WORLD!

1. Donuts (USA)
2. Aborrajados (Colombia)
3. Bomboloni (Italy)
4. Krapfen (Germany)
5. Polish Donuts (Poland)
6. Mandazi (Kenya and Tanzania)
7. Pisang Goreng (Indonesia)

Countries and **cultures** around the world have their own unique and traditional desserts. Their ingredients and techniques can be similar to or very different from one another.

MAKING CONNECTIONS

TEXT-TO-SELF

Do you like deep-fried desserts? If so, what is your favorite kind?

TEXT-TO-TEXT

Have you read any other books about food from around the world? What did you learn in those books that was not in this one?

TEXT-TO-WORLD

What are some other ways, besides dessert, that countries and cultures from around the world are special and different from one another?

GLOSSARY

crises — situations that are not stable or certain, usually causing a great deal of stress.

culture — the language, customs, ideas, and art of a particular group of people.

debuted — presented to the public for the first time.

fast — to eat very little or no food for religious or political reasons.

fritter — a piece of fried dough, often containing bits of fruit, vegetables, meat, or fish, and shaped into a small cake.

milestone — an important event or turning point in history or in a person's life.

scored — to have a line made in something using a sharp instrument.

shepherd — a person who herds and watches over sheep.

INDEX

Ancient Egyptians, 4
Ancient Romans, 5

Bambalouni, 22–23
Beaver Tail, 18–19
Beignet, 10, 13

Canada, 18
Churro, 14

England, 7

France, 10, 13

India, 26

Jalebi, 26–27
Japan, 23

Korea, 20
Korean Twisted Donut, 20

Mardi Gras, 13
Mesopotamians, 4
Mochi Donut, 23

Persia, 7
Peru, 16
Picaron, 16–17
Puff Puff, 24–25

Spain, 14

Tunisia, 22

United States, 13

West Africa, 24

DiscoverRoo!
ONLINE RESOURCES

This book is filled with videos, puzzles, games, and more! Scan the QR codes* while you read, or visit the website below to make this book pop.

popbooksonline.com/deep-fried

*Scanning QR codes requires a web-enabled smart device with a QR code reader app and a camera.